Safety Zone:
Scriptural Prayers to
Revolutionize Your School

by

Nancy Huff

ISBN 978-1500 743765

What Others Are Saying....

"Nancy Huff has done an extraordinary job in high-lighting prayer for our schools. Many Christians today are realizing that we need intercession for our schools and this is an excellent and needed resource!"
Cindy Jacobs, Generals International

"I am excited about this book, **"Safety Zone: Scriptural Prayers to Revolutionize Your School"** by Nancy Huff. Children today are tomorrow's leaders. What will be their educational foundation? We have already seen the fulfillment of Abraham Lincoln's words, "The philosophy of the schoolroom in one generation will be the philosophy of government in the next."
Isaiah 9:7 says, 'There will be no end to the increase of His government or of peace, on the throne of David and over his kingdom, To establish it and to uphold it with justice and righteousness from then on and forevermore. The zeal of the LORD of hosts will accomplish this.'

It is time for us to unite as The Body of Christ-His Ekklesia and take back what the Devil has stolen! Just as the Lord gave Israel the whole promise land but then had them advance piece by piece as they could maintain what they had claimed, this book is designed to help us do the same thing. It is time for us to secure a 'Spiritual Safety Zone' around every school in America and penetrate the Education System with the Zeal of the Lord in Prayer."

**Dr. John Benefiel,
Heartland Apostolic Prayer Network**

All Scripture is God-breathed and is useful

for teaching, rebuking, correcting and

training in righteousness.

2 Timothy 3:16

Contents

Contents

Dedication

This book is dedicated to Donna Sams.

Over the years, Donna has spent countless hours prayer-walking schools. She has prayed for thousands of children whose names she will never know and whose faces she will never see this side of eternity. She is a true intercessor who loves Jesus with all her heart.

Introduction

Many people would agree that the modern American educational system is in deep trouble. Our school system is like a huge donkey that continues to sit on our kitchen table and everyone ignores it because no one knows what to do about it. The only time we want to address the problems is when the news media shocks us with coverage of yet another school shooting or another teacher being arrested for molesting a student. Parents, grandparents, teachers, and students who are directly involved in the day-to-day school activities know full well the extent of the problem, but they often must ignore the donkey because someone higher up or older than they have allowed the donkey in and given him permission to sit on the table. Because of the daily battles in the classrooms, they know better than anyone that all is not well.

Across the nation we're facing the problems of declining test scores, watered down curriculum, a decrease in school attendance, and students who graduate without learning to read, just to name a few. Then there are the moral issues within the school walls—abortion, bullying, cheating, teachers having sex with their students, and school shootings. The problems run like a giant octopus whose tentacles reach even to the smallest community in our country. The usual approaches to the problems—spending more money and adding new guidelines and laws, for instance—are not working. It's obvious that the system is in trouble, but no one knows what to do about it.

For the most part, as believers we either take our children out of the system and place them in home schools or private schools, or we stand on the sidelines and pray for our own children as they face huge temptations the likes of which their grandparents never dreamed. Even many of those who have no children in school are aware of the decline in the individual integrity of our nation.

As a former teacher in both public and private schools, I have seen the problems and the progress of decline firsthand. I believe that behind all the sin and turmoil in our educational system there is a force of evil bidding for the minds and souls of our children and ultimately our nation. When schools originally were established in America, the Word of God was taught as truth, along with the teaching and precepts of Jesus Christ. Few people are aware that the American educational system was set on a negative spiritual course over 100 years ago that has produced the manifestation of decline that we experience in our schools nowadays. We must realize that if a spirit of deception is behind the scenes, that spirit can be displaced and replaced by the living God, who longs to heal and transform. He is waiting on us to take our place in faith and believe Him for change.

So what do we do? I contend that now is the time for the church to arise like never before in history and begin to pray and believe God for a turnaround in our educational system, which is why I have written this book. It is not too late—it is just the perfect time for an army of believers to come forth.

Often we hear the argument, "These are the last days and 2 Timothy 3 tells us that there will be godlessness in the last days, so things are just going to get worse and worse until the Lord returns." That is no excuse for letting the enemy run over our children and our nation. Lou Engle, the minister who helped to found International House of Prayer in Kansas City, Missouri, and who sponsors "The Call" that fills stadiums with youth who pray for this nation, has said, "Don't think that because it is the last days we have to put up with evil!" It is not too late and we as believers must never give up!

Creating Godly Change

Sometimes all it takes is one person who will step out and believe God for change. A wonderful example is William Wilberforce, who in 1780 was elected to the English House of Commons at the age of twenty-one. England's culture was in a dismal downward spiral with no hope of redemption. Almost all of the English economy was based on slavery, debtor's prisons were common, child labor was the norm, and education was nonexistent for most children. The poor accepted their lot of long hours of hard manual labor and the elite loved their life of partying and gaiety, often at the expense of the poor and the enslaved. On October 28, 1787, Wilberforce wrote in his diary the words that have now become famous: "God Almighty has set before me two great objects, the suppression of the Slave Trade and the Reformation of Manners." Wilberforce realized that unless the hearts of the people were changed, slavery could not be eradicated—the change in manners (culture) went hand-in-hand with the abolition of the slave trade.

The genius of the plan given to Wilberforce for creating a godly change in his nation is that it's applicable to us today in changing our school system. Wilberforce gathered like- minded people around him who would dream of what England could be like if it were a moral society. Wilberforce referred to their meetings as "The Better Hour"—that time of the day spent with his friends, praying and dreaming.

So what would happen today if small groups of people came together to dream of what our educational system would be like if it were transformed by God's grace? Maybe, just maybe, God would use these small groups gathered around Him and His Word to change every school in this nation. That is my dream and the catalyst for putting together this little book of prayers.

It is my desire that there would be small groups all over this nation—one group in every school—who would be willing to pray both individually and together and to believe God for miracles in the hearts and lives of the students, teachers, support staff, and administrators of their schools. Then they would see the "big picture" and begin to pray for the organizations that govern the schools, such as their local and state school boards, the National Department of Education, and the National Educational Association.

This little prayer book is meant to instill dreams of great cultural change that would be possible when two or more people come together in the name of our Lord Jesus and believe Him to transform a nation's educational system. It was through Wilberforce's individual effort—along with the encouragement, support, and prayers of his friends— that slavery was finally abolished and the culture changed in his country. So this book of prayers was written for individual as well as group prayer because even one person who will pray can make a difference. It wouldn't have to be the elite or the powerful but just people who have faith in God and would believe Him when He said, **"If you ask anything in My name, I will do it" (John 14:14 NKJV).**

Step Out and Believe

For years, Teach the Children International, the nonprofit organization I founded in 1998, had people who would prayer walk around a school and pray for that school. There were tremendous testimonies of divine protection and intervention that occurred. One interesting observation is that most of the prayer walkers were adults who had no children in the school for which they were praying. They just had a heart to see God move. Because of those prayers, school shootings were averted and children were spared.

Let us put aside our passiveness and take up the challenge that God is giving us to take our nation one school at a time. This is not the hour to give in to evil and rest in the fact that the Lord is coming back and we hope that it is soon to deliver us from all the evil in this world. The trouble with that ideology is that if we live only to look for His return we are likely to be the person who is hit by a Greyhound bus from behind (so to speak). God is expecting us to look both ways—for Him to change the world in which we live as well as to look for His return. We must also remember that it has taken over 100 years of our faulty decisions that have caused our schools to be humanistic. They will not be changed in a day.

I realize that t written prayers are not always the best because it is easy to read the words with no breath (power) of the Holy Spirit behind them. They become empty rituals that produce no fruit of answered prayer. I believe that the prayers in this book have been divinely inspired and written out to give depth to your prayers. Yet, another reason for praying powerless prayers may be a lack of knowledge.

I have attended many prayer meetings where the prayers seem to never go beyond the surface because of the lack of knowledge on the subject. For example, how many people think to pray for the National Education Association (NEA) when they pray for our schools? Yet the NEA is a major stronghold over all the educational system in this country. The NEA was originally set up to help teachers get together and share teaching techniques and networking for teachers. Then in the early 1900s, it became the vehicle that promoted a humanist agenda that has brought about the change in our system with which we are dealing presently. The NEA is one area that should never be neglected in our prayer time for our schools.

It is my hope that you will use this prayer book as "a jumping off point," that the prayers will lead you into deeper areas of education that need prayer covering. By all means, let the Holy Spirit lead you in the prayers that He has for the time, the place, and the situation in which you find yourself, your children, and the children of this nation.

May God bless you as you take up His charge to pray and believe!

> **"From the days of John the Baptist until now, the kingdom of heaven has been forcefully advancing, and forceful men lay hold of it.!"**
> **Matthew 11:12 NIV**

Prayers for—Protection for Our Children

Prayer for a Protective Blood Line

"The Lord said there are enough believers in every town to take back our schools. The plan is that two people each morning, before school starts, will circle the school and draw a blood line around it..."
Rachel Tefateller – Prophecy at Billy Brim Prayer Gathering 2000

Father, I draw a blood line of Your protection around this school. I ask for Your protection for everyone in this building. Just as the blood on the doorpost of the children of Israel signified that inside the house, the Death Angel would have to pass over that house and not enter in to take the life of the firstborn son; I ask now that the blood line I am putting around this school by applying Your Son's blood with my words would cause the Angel of Death to pass over everyone in this school.

Let no harmful weapon, or death-producing anger enter these hallways. Let every hidden plot of the enemy that would kill, steal, or destroy be revealed. I ask that You, who came to give abundant life, flood the halls, classrooms, cafeteria, offices, and every other area with Your presence.

As Jesus shed His blood so that we might be free, I ask that You set the people in this school free from the bondages of sin—deliver the students and the staff from fear, dangerous and damaging anger, homosexuality, promiscuousness, and every evil deed. Amen

Scripture References:
Exodus 12:13
Isaiah 54:17
John 10:7–10
1 Corinthians 4:5
Galatians 5:1
1 John 2:14

Prayer for Protection from Disaster

And though this world, with devils filled, should
threaten to undo us,
We will not fear, for God has willed His truth to
triumph through us;
The Prince of Darkness grim, we tremble not for him;
His rage we can endure, For lo! His doom is sure;
One little word shall fell him.
Martin Luther

Lord, I stand as an intercessor on behalf of this school so that it will not be destroyed nor will the students or staff be harmed. I ask You for Your protective power to be present here. Give Your charge over this school to keep it safe in all its ways.

I pray that You will hide these students in Your shelter; You will be their stronghold in time of trouble; You will help and deliver them from the wicked because they take refuge in You. You are our help and strength, an ever-present help in times of trouble.

Father, when Your people have suffered because of disaster, let them turn back to You. If we, as Your children, have sinned and a disaster has come because of that sin, let us confess Your name and pray to You. Then You will hear from heaven and forgive our sin and bring us back into Your presence. Amen.

Scripture References:

Genesis 18:20–33

Psalm 9:9

Psalm 27:5

Psalm 46:1

Psalm 59:16

Proverbs 11:8

Nahum 1:7

John 16:33

2 Chronicles 6:23–40

Psalm 10:14

Psalm 37:39

Psalm 50:15

Psalm 91:15

Ezekiel 22:30

Matthew 13:21

Romans 8:35

Prayer for Protection from Terrorists

You are to plan for offensive, in your headquarters you will never think defensively.
Winston Churchill to Lord Mountbatten in World War II

Lord Jesus, I come to our strong tower, the name of Jesus, and ask for protection for this school and every person and family represented here. I ask for divine intervention regarding any plan of any terrorist that would want to come here to kill, steal, or destroy the lives of those in this school. Reveal those things that are hidden and make every clandestine act planned or talked about be thwarted.

I ask that You guard over the doors and windows of this building that no harm could befall anyone that has anything to do with this institution. Let the innocence of our children not be a lure for the evil that is in this world. I bind all powers and principalities that have been given assignment over this area, and I render them helpless in the Name of Jesus. Amen.

Scripture References:
Psalm 91   Proverbs 28:10
Daniel 2:22   John 10:10
Ephesians 6:12

Prayer for Protection from Pedophiles

God has not promised that the whole world would be saved by prayer,
But undoubtedly there are many situations that would be totally changed by the amassing of the prayer of God's preserving intercessors.
Wesley L. Duewel – <u>Mighty Prevailing Prayer</u>

Father, I come before You and ask that You keep evil men and women away from this school. I bind all powers and principalities that would draw men or women to even look at any child associated with this institution. Expose any evil intent before anyone has a chance to cause harm to a child whether it be here, in their homes, churches, after-school programs, or social events.

Give the children discernment as to those who mean to cause them harm. Surround the children with Your angels. Amen.

Scripture References:
Psalm 91
Proverbs 3:21–22
Matthew 18:19
2 Thessalonians 3:2
1 Peter 3:22

Prayer for Protection from Vandalism

It is the sin of our silence when we should speak up that
makes cowards of us all.
Martin Luther King

Lord, I know there are some who would want to bring harm to this school building that You have provided, and so I ask that You protect this property and everything in it. I pray that those who are filled with anger would find You and know Your peace in their hearts.

Expose any evil intent aimed at destruction. May every child who has overheard any destructive plan report that plan to the authorities. Let those in authority take note of what was shared with them and let them take proper action.

You have set before each person life, prosperity, death, and destruction. We ask that each person choose life and prosperity not death and destruction. Amen.

Scripture References:
Deuteronomy 30:15
Proverbs 29:22
1 Corinthians 4:5

Prayer Against Acts of Violence

A juvenile offense at ages 6-11 is the strongest predictor of subsequent violence or serious delinquency even if the offense did not involve violence. America's Youth: measuring the risk by the Institute for Youth Development

Father, in the Name of Jesus, I come to You and ask for Your protection for this school from acts of violence. I ask, first of all, that any violent or evil agenda that is being planned against the students, educators, and support staff in this school be revealed. Nothing in all creation is hidden from Your sight; everything is uncovered and laid bare before You. Let no weapon enter the premises of this building.

May the protection that the blood of Jesus provides be stronger here than any evil that man or child could imagine.

Let those students who have a propensity to steal, kill, and destroy be like the madman who lived in the tombs in the region of the Gerasenes. Let them know the power and the deliverance of our Lord Jesus Christ. I ask for godly help for each troubled child.

May the emotional needs of the children be met in their families so they will have a strong moral background and Godly character. Amen.

Scripture References:
Isaiah 54:17
Psalm 5:5–6
Psalm 5:9
Mark 5:1–20
Luke 4:33-37
Romans 8:35–9:1
Ephesians 6:14–19
1 Timothy 5:8
Hebrews 4:12–13
Hebrews 11:7

Prayer for Those in Gangs or Those Being Pursued by Gangs

We do well to ask God to help us discern the invisible spiritual forces that are behind the visible problems in the city. John Dawson – <u>Warfare Prayer</u>

Father, I come to You as an intercessor on behalf of those students who are involved with a gang or who are being pressured to become a part of a gang. I ask that You reveal Yourself to them. Be a father to those who need a father. Send those who will comfort those who need comforting. Send godly friends to those who need friends.

Send laborers into this school to minister to those who need the security and acceptance of a gang. Let them know that they are accepted in Your Kingdom—just as they are. Let the believers dispel the demons that are active here, and when the believers place their hands on the students, they will get well.

Expose those who are trying to promote gang activity.

I ask that the spirit of fear be dispelled, and instead there would be a spirit of power, love, and a sound mind.

I address the powers and principalities over this school, and I say "You have no part in any student here. You must go, in the mighty Name of Jesus." Amen.

Scripture References:
Proverbs 28:5
Luke 7:34
1 Corinthians 4:5
Ephesians 6:12
2 Timothy 1:17

Prayer to Stop School Shootings

We would still be having serious difficulties in our schools if the professionals did everything right. Why? Because what goes on in the classroom cannot be separated from the problems occurring in culture and families at large.
Dr. James Dobson – "Focus on the Family Magazine"

Father, I come to You asking for Your protection for everyone in this school. If there is anyone here who is contemplating murder, I pray that they would be stopped and that godly people would be able to minister to them at their point of need. I know that the weapons we fight with are not the weapons of this world, so I bind any evil principalities and powers over this school that would want to steal, kill, or destroy the lives of the students, teachers, administrators, and support staff. Let all plans of evil be exposed before it can be consummated.

I thank You for the power of God—that Your power is loosed over this school and that no evil will befall anyone in this school.

I ask for a complete moral and spiritual revival in America. And when that revival comes, I pray that it would change the hearts and minds of our children so that no child would ever think of killing someone else. Amen.

Scripture References:
Exodus 20:13   Psalm 91:10–13
1 Timothy 1:5–11   1 Timothy 1:18–19
1 Peter 3:9–12

Prayer for Those Contemplating Suicide

So a son believes the lie of that beguiling death and
yields himself to its enticing snares and finds respite
and false calls of "Peace, peace" –
And a child turns aside from a hopeless future into a
cold, dark death that quickly devours the life of that
son and then laughs loud and long in the face of my
God whose heritage is the children...
Dr. Patricia Morgan <u>Tell Me Again – The Cry of the</u>
<u>Children</u>

Dear heavenly Father, You know those who have thoughts of death and ending their lives. I ask that You shine Your light on those children. Show them how special they are in Your kingdom. Let them find You as the source of life and their reason for living. Where there is hate let there be love. Protect them on days that they are particularly vulnerable.

I bind the spirit of death over them, and I come against all rejection that has been aimed at them either intentionally or unintentionally. Give them the strength of God in their spirits to stand against the enemy when he whispers to them that death is the only way out of their situation, and that no one cares. Show them You care.

Send laborers to them to treat them with kindness. Let a teacher compliment them. Let students around them follow the Golden Rule. Amen.

Scripture References:
Matthew 18:18–19
John 3:16
Romans 8:31–36
Romans 15:7
Ephesians 3:16
Luke 10:2
Luke 6:31

Prayer to Dispel Fear

Sure I must fight, if I would reign;
increase my courage, Lord;
I'll bear the toil, endure the pain,
supported by Thy word.
Isaac Watts – Hymn "Am I a Soldier of the
Cross?"

Father, I come to You on behalf of the teachers in our schools. So often they walk a tightrope, not knowing what they can say or do.

Create an open heaven over this school that the teachers, students, administrators, and support staff would not be intimidated when they talk about their faith in You. You, Father, have not given them the spirit of fear, but of love and of self-discipline. Let the teachers and administrators not shrink back from reaching out to their students, but let them walk in great wisdom and understanding. Keep them in Your protection and under Your watchful eye.

I bind a spirit of fear, and I ask for wisdom, love, and boldness. May the students, teachers, and administrators walk in a godly fear of You. Amen.

Scripture References:
Deuteronomy 6:13
Matthew 18:19
Deuteronomy 10:12–13
2 Timothy 1:7

2 Chronicles 15:9
1 John 4:18
Proverbs 8:13

Prayer for Protection

*...the unerring hand of Providence is always active
amidst the shower of Balls, Bombs, and rockets...*
Andrew Jackson

Lord Jesus, I plead the blood of Jesus over this school and
ask that You give Your angels charge over this building and
everyone who enters the premises. Deliver everyone in this
school from evil and harm. Let Your kingdom come in this
place. Expose all the evil works of darkness before any of the
plans of Satan can be carried out against the children,
teachers, and support staff. I ask that You protect and rescue
them.

Give an open door to the Gospel of Jesus and let the light of
Your glory come to this school. I ask this in the mighty
Name of Jesus. Amen.

Scripture References:
Psalm 91
Isaiah 54:17
Matthew 6:13
Hebrews 4:12–13

Prayers for—Educational Organizations

Prayer for the NEA
(National Education Association)

Are American teachers being trained and manipulated by the NEA to bring socialism to America? If they are, then the NEA is little more than the socialists Trojan horse within our political walls.
Samuel L. Blumfenfeld <u>NEA – Trojan Horse in American Education</u>

Father, I lift up the leaders of the NEA and I ask that first of all, if any of them do not know You as their personal Lord and Savior, that You send laborers into their path to share the Good News of the Gospel with them.

I ask that the NEA leaders make wise and godly decisions that would benefit the children of this nation.

Expose any ungodly agenda set forth by the NEA. I ask that all ungodly influence be stopped and that Your people would be firm in recognizing policies and agendas that are against Your Word. Let Your people be as watchmen on the wall day and night crying out to You on behalf of the students of this land. Let no one who intends evil prevail. Let Your people be firm in their knowledge of You and quick to recognize when truth is not proclaimed.

Unite the Christians and let them be one in spirit as they seek better ways to make the NEA an organization that will glorify You. Let the NEA become a beacon of light and a help to those who are educators. Let their money be spent for programs that profit the children and not for political influence. Turn the heart of the leaders of the NEA toward the teachers and the students. Let the NEA create godly curriculum and learning programs that will make our students want to learn and excel in all knowledge and wisdom. Amen.

Scripture References:

Psalm 26:4–8	Psalm 78:5–8
Psalm109:2–5	Psalm 127:1
Isaiah 55:2	Isaiah 62:6–7
Ezekiel 11:21	Luke 6:43–45
Ephesians 4:14–15	1 Timothy 2:1–7
1 Timothy 2:1–2	Hebrews 3:12–14
2 John 7–9	

Prayer for PTO
(Parent-Teacher Organizations)

*Sometimes you don't have to go very far to go a long
way toward transforming a city.*
Steve Hawthorne and Grahm Kendrick

Father, I thank You that the PTO will not be yoked with
ungodly agendas. Instead, they will follow after Your heart
for their children and the schools, and You will be their God
and they will be Your people. They will separate themselves
from ungodly programs that lead our children away from
You. I pray that they will have a heart for their children. I ask
that You give them a voice that they will speak forth the truth
and they will produce fruit of righteousness and not
unrighteousness.

Raise up godly parents who have a heart for You, who will
interface with schools for the good of the children. I pray that
they will adopt policies and programs that lift You up and
provide a moral compass for our children. I pray for
repentance among the leadership, that they will repent from
promoting godless programs of sex education and humanism.

Restore this organization to the intent that You ordained and
let them come along beside the schools and provide services
that will increase godliness and learning. Amen.

Scripture References:
Joshua 1:6–9
Jeremiah 15:19
Matthew 3:7–9
2 Corinthians 6:14–18

Isaiah 59:19–21
Malachi 4:6
Romans 12:2
James 3:3–12

Prayer for the National Department of Education

O watch and fight, and pray.
The battle ne'er give o'er.
The work of faith will not be done,
Til thou obtain thy crown.
Fight on, my soul... Hymn by George Heath

Dear heavenly Father, I come before You on behalf of the National Department of Education. I pray that as long as this department exists it will make godly decisions on behalf of the children of this land. I pray for accountability for the money given to them. As they are faithful in little, let them increase.

May all the programs they institute be for the benefit of the children of this land and keep them away from fruitless efforts. I ask that no godless, vain plans come out of the Department of Education but only that which edifies and raises the educational standards of America.

Let only those with a servant's heart work in this organization. Keep away all those who would be hirelings. Raise up godly leadership that will lead in all godliness and righteousness.

I ask You to bless this organization and thank You that You keep the National Department of Education free from evil as they seek and pursue peace and turn from all deceitfulness. I pray this in Jesus precious Name. Amen.

Scripture References:
Psalm 2:1–6
Proverbs 29:2
Luke 16:10–13
John 10:11–13
1 Peter 3:9–12

Prayer for the Local School Boards

You will never aspire to pray until you urge and force yourselves. John Calvin

Dear heavenly Father, I pray for godly men and women of influence who will run and be elected for school board positions in this school district. Give us men and women of integrity who know Your way and Your Word and who are willing to step into a position of influence in our schools. Let them not shrink back from the battle that wages for the souls of our children. Let them have the backbone to stand up for Christian values and principles. Let them be proactive and sacrificial in their zeal for implementing godly principles in this school.

I pray for those who are Christians and godly who may already be serving as school board members. Give them favor with administrators, teachers, negotiators, and support personnel. You said in Your Word that if a man's ways please You, You would make him walk in peace. May those who stand up for Your Word and Your ethics have favor with God and man.

I pray for moral purity in those who are in authority and that their families would be in order. Let them make godly decisions based on Your Word and not on man's reasoning or political correctness.

May our schools be transformed on every level, not just in the classroom, but also in the school board meetings.

I thank You and I pray in the Name of Jesus. Amen.

Scripture References:
1 Chronicles 11:10–14
Proverbs 16:7
1 Corinthians 2:4–5

Prayers for—Students

Prayer for Classroom Discipline

Whatever makes men good Christians, makes them good citizens. Daniel Webster

Father, I pray for orderliness in the classroom. Let the children love instruction and knowledge. Give the teachers and administration disciplinary strategies that work. Let the students see education as a privilege and not as drudgery. Thank You that the peace of God that passes all understanding will keep the hearts and minds of everyone in the classroom. I pray that children who choose to be disruptive will be disciplined.

Let the administration and the parents support of the teachers in the classrooms be to the extent that when a child is sent in for discipline he or she will receive proper consequences for unacceptable behavior.

Give the teachers emotional stability so they will discipline in love and understanding. Channel the children with learning difficulties so they will receive the proper help and will not be a source of confusion or disruption in the classroom.

I bind all hindering spirits that would keep learning from happening in this building and I ask that the angels of heaven be released to care for and protect everyone here. Expose any hidden works of darkness that need exposure. Shine Your light on those who are in need of a loving word or touch and give the teachers sensitivity to the need of that student.

Grant Your wisdom for every teacher to know how to handle each situation. In Jesus Name I pray. Amen.

Scripture References:

Psalm 91:9–13

Proverbs 22:10

Matthew 16:19

1 Corinthians 14:40

Philippians 4:6–7

James 1:6

Proverbs 6:23

Proverbs 23:12–14

1 Corinthians 4:5

Ephesians 6:10–13

1 Peter 5:7–8

Prayer for Those with Learning Challenges

If a man's eye is on the Eternal, his intellect will grow. Ralph Waldo Emerson

Dear heavenly Father, I thank You that You have made everything perfect in Your eyes. You do not make mistakes. Now I ask that You help each child in this school who has difficulty learning. Let Your Word be in their hearts and minds that they may meditate in it day and night. Then You will make their way prosperous and successful. Let them rely on You and You will be made strong in their weaknesses.

Guide their paths. Give them teachers who are wise and full of patience, grace, and mercy. Let them depend on You for their every need and may You show Yourself strong on their behalf. Make the simple wise and let their learning not be a source of pride but may it rest on Your power.

I ask for encouragement for every child with learning challenges. Give them strength when insults, hardships, persecution, and difficulties come their way. Amen.

Scripture References:

2 Chronicles 16:9

Psalm 19:7

Romans 8:26

2 Corinthians 12:9

Joshua 1:7–9

Isaiah 30:19–21

1 Corinthians 2:4–5

Hebrews 4:14–16

Prayer for Those Who Are Being Bullied

Tell me again how all that suffering, and all that abuse, and all that crying Will be swallowed up in the victory songs of first-fruit sons. And the rich harvest of manifested sons and the mourning will turn into dancing...
Tell me again. Dr. Patricia Morgan <u>Tell Me Again-The Cry of the Children</u>

Father, let each child be confident in who he or she is in Christ Jesus. I ask that for cursing there would be blessing, for bullying there would be admonition, for hate there would be Your love; that evil would not overcome good but good would prevail.

I pray on behalf of the students who may feel insecure and those who are hurt by the words of those who feel they have power over them. I stand as an intercessor and pray Your love on them. I bless them because You said that in the face of cursing we should bless. I turn the other cheek on behalf of those who are weak. I ask that You allow Your children to do good to them that persecute the weaker children; that there would be a great reward for those who follow Your Word, and that mercy would prevail because You are a merciful God. Amen.

Scripture References:
Proverbs 22:10
Luke 6:27–31
1 Thessalonians 5:15

Proverbs 25:21–22
Romans 12:14–21

Prayer for Academic Excellence

The secret of my success? It is simple. It is found in the Bible, "In all thy ways acknowledge Him and He shall direct thy paths." George Washington Carver

Father, I ask for academic excellence in this school. Let the students have reasoning ability and understanding on the material being taught. Let them have wisdom to see beyond what they see with their eyes and hear with their ears.

Enable the teachers to make the material relevant and easily understood.

I ask that the lifestyles of the families be such that learning would increase. Let the children eat healthy food and get plenty of rest so they will be able to comprehend what is being taught. I pray for good study habits and a renewed interest in doing homework, and that the test scores would reflect these changes.

I pray that the students will embrace wisdom and in all their getting they will get understanding. Let them acknowledge You, God, as their Creator and the Source of all wisdom and understanding.

Father, I pray that this country will realize that the minds of its children are the greatest resource we have. Amen.

Scripture References:
Genesis 41:14–16
Proverbs 4:7–13
Daniel 1:12–20

Psalm 14:1
Isaiah 11:1–4
Daniel 5:12

Prayer for Godly Use of Technology

Teachers, not technology should teach.
SCANS Report 2000 U.S. Department of Education

Father, I pray over the computers in this school. I pray that You will keep the children here away from those who are treacherous, rash, conceited, and lovers of pleasure rather than lovers of God—particularly those who use computers for evil purposes.

I pray that the children will flee from evil and will desire to serve You rather than Satan. I ask that You expose those evil persons who would promote pornography and sensual material on the Internet, and deliver those children and teachers who are already ensnared by the trap of the devil.

Reveal the hidden things of darkness. Let the fear of God come on this place in such a way that the children would flee from the evil that would enslave them through the ungodly use computers. In Jesus Name I pray. Amen.

Scripture References:
Psalm 25:15   Psalm 91:3
Psalm 119:110   Psalms 124:7–125:1
Psalm 140:4–5   2 Timothy 3:1–6
2 Timothy 3:13   1 Corinthians 4:5

Prayers for—Educators

Prayer for Teachers

He who opens a school door, closes a prison. Victor Hugo

Father, I ask that You give each teacher a discerning heart to be able to guide his/her classroom. Give the ability to distinguish between right and wrong so they will be an example in purity, word, and deed to the students they teach.

I pray that the teachers would not be hirelings but shepherds who will guide the children as tender sheep.

Let the teachers be strong disciplinarians and also filled with the fruit of the Spirit in love, joy, peace, patience, kindness, goodness, faithfulness, gentleness, and self-control. I pray that the children would be provoked to do good works and to learn. I ask that the teachers will be kind to everyone and gently instruct so that the students will come to the knowledge of the truth and not be ensnared by the devil's tactics.

Reveal those things to the teachers that they need to know. Let the sensitivity of the Holy Spirit be present in every encounter with the children. Amen.

Scripture References:
1 Kings 3:7–9   John 10:1–6
Galatians 5:22–26   2 Timothy 2:23–3:1

Prayer for Administrators

Providence has given to our people the choice of their rulers. And it is the duty as well as the privilege and interest, of a Christian nation to select and prefer Christians for their rulers.
First Chief Justice of Supreme Court, John Jay

Dear heavenly Father, I lift up to You the administrators in this school. I ask for godly men and women to fill those positions. And if there are any here who do not know You as their personal Savior, I ask that You reveal Yourself to them and send laborers to them to give them a godly witness of Your plan of eternal salvation for their lives. I ask for administrators who are called to be shepherds for the children under their care and not administrators who are hirelings.

You told us to ask for wisdom and I ask for wisdom for those rendering decisions for the students. Let that wisdom be pure, peace-loving, considerate, submissive, full of mercy and good fruit, impartial, and sincere. Let all decisions be done justly and with fairness. Where strong discipline is needed, I pray that You give them the strength to stand strong, even when that discipline will produce negative criticism. Give them parental support with their wise decisions.

Help each administrator to cast all their care on You because You care for them.

Let their families be strong and supportive of the jobs You have called them to do.

I pray that intercessors will rise up who will lift up this administration and be faithful to stand in the gap for them as they shepherd the children in this school. Amen.

Scripture References:

Jeremiah 1:17–2:1

Micah 6:8

John 10:12–13

James 1:6

Ezekiel 22:31

Luke 10:2

1 Peter 5:1–4,7

James 3:17–18

Prayer for Counselors

The God we believe in is One who protects the
children, empowers the elderly, and walks
with working men and women. As Christians,
we wish to act accordingly. We believe you
share in similar concerns. Let us join hands.
R. Fung – The Isaiah Vision: An Ecumenical Strategy
for Congregational Evangelism

Dear heavenly Father, I come to You asking for wisdom for
the counselors in this school. When families and students
come to them for help, let them give godly council. Let Your
Word be the standard for all guidance. Give the counselors
great discernment and let them see beyond what they see
with their eyes and hear with their ears.

Give the counselors a good rapport with the students and
their families. Let families come to them for help knowing
that they will receive the answers they need for the problems
they face with their children.

I pray that the counselors in this school will not encourage
sexual activity among the students, abortions for the young
girls, and all other forms of ungodly behavior that will hurt
the students and their families and bring curses on this land.
Instead, the counselors will hate evil and love Your Law.

I remind You of Your Word where You said that if we come
to You and have acted foolishly that You would forgive us
and heal our wounds. I ask for Your healing power to be
released in this place—healing from emotional wounds,

physical wounds, and spiritual wounds. Let the counselor's office be a place of refuge and comfort. Let the strength that comes from godly counsel be administered with love and understanding.

Refresh the souls of those counselors who are tired and who are weary in their jobs. Let them know Your strength and Your determination to be a helper to those who are in need. Give them the heart of the good Samaritan that they will bind up the wounds and take those who are hurting to a safe haven.

Render just decisions for the poor and the needy and let counselors speak up for those who cannot speak for themselves. Let them be a voice for the voiceless. Amen.

Scripture References:
Job 12:13
Proverbs 31:8–9
Psalm 1:1
Psalm 97:10
1 Peter 2:1–4
Psalm 107:17–29
Proverbs 4:10–11

Luke 10:30–35
Psalm 25:4–5
John 16:14
Psalm 73:23–24
Psalm 119:105
Proverbs 8:13–14

Prayer for Support Staff

Prayer burden begins as an inner impression that you should pray for a known or unknown need. The burden is the Spirit's personal call to you to intercede.
Wesley L. Duewel – <u>Mighty Prevailing Prayer</u>

Dear Lord Jesus, I thank You for all those who work in the schools as support staff—those who tend the offices, drive the buses, cook the food, provide security, and clean the halls. I ask that You give each one a wise and discerning heart as they work so that no evil person or evil deed could get past their watchful eyes. I ask that they be praised when praise is due and that their jobs are deemed important as they make the school run smoothly.

Let them be dependable and trustworthy and full of kind and encouraging words as they deal with the students. Let there be no gossip and dissension among them but rather let the fruit of the Spirit be evident in their lives. If there are any here who do not know You as their personal Savior, let them meet You as their Savior and Lord. I ask this in the Name of Jesus. Amen.

Scripture References:
1 Samuel 30:23
Proverbs 6:6–8
Proverbs 13:17
Isaiah 54:16
Galatians 5:22–26

Proverbs 3:21–26
Proverbs 11:13
Proverbs 14:35
Acts 13:22

Prayers for—
Extracurricular Activities

Prayer for Safety over Sports Activities

It has long since come to my attention that people of accomplishment rarely sat back and let things happen to them. They went out and happened to things. Elinor Smith

Dear heavenly Father, I ask that You watch over every child involved in this sports event and that You protect each of them from injury and harm.

I pray that each participant and spectator will exhibit good sportsmanship. Let those who lose learn from their mistakes and may those who win not be haughty or proud. May good, fair, and honest competition take place, and may this event build character in each of the players.

I ask that no one would use Your name in vain. Let strong moral character be displayed in every word and deed.

I ask for safety for everyone observing this event. Reveal any plot of anyone who would want to come in to cause harm to any participant or spectator and let that evil intent be dealt with by the proper authorities.

I pray that the coaches, judges, and umpires be impartial in all their judgments. Let a godly witness of Your ability to save, redeem, and sustain Your people be shown in team members, officials, coaches, parents, and observers.

And, Lord, I pray that You bless every student on both teams and that anyone who doesn't know You as Savior and Lord will come into that relationship with You. Amen.

Scripture References:
Isaiah 65:23
Psalm 32:7
Psalm 91:14–15
1 Corinthians 9:27–10:1
Jude 24
Revelation 1:1

Prayer for Ministries That Work with Children

Jesus loves me! He who died,
Heaven's gate to open wide;
He will wash away my sin,
Let His little Child come in. Hymn – Jesus Loves Me

Lord, I lift up the ministries that work with the children in this school. I ask that You give each organization—whether it is a church youth group, a para-church organization, or a club—wisdom and insight into effective means of reaching children with the Gospel of Jesus Christ. May each ministry come in the power and the demonstration of the Holy Spirit so that children, parents, and teachers would be drawn to the love of God. Let the hearts and minds of the children be open to receive the message of Jesus.

I ask that You meet all the material and financial needs of these ministries.

I pray for laborers to come to the organizations. I pray for leaders who have the best interest of the children in their hearts.

I ask that the children be kept safe while they are in the care of these ministries. Amen.

Scripture References:
Psalm 140:1
2 Corinthians 4: 3–4

Mark 16:15–18
Philippians 4:19

Prayer for Bible Clubs in Schools

In the lands beyond the sea,
countless million children be who have never heard the
gospel story told:
Little ones for whom the Christ died, and bo't them with a
price,
waiting to be gathered in the Savior's fold.
Hymn – Jesus Loves the Children by Thoro Harris

Dear heavenly Father, I pray that if there is not a Bible club in this school that You would lay it on someone's heart to start a club. For the ones that already exist and for those that may start, I ask that the Word of God become alive to the children.

Give the workers new and innovative ways to share the truth of Your Word so that the children would hide Your Word in their hearts that they would be able to resist sin.

Grant the clubs favor with the administration.

Let the children be trained in the way they should go and when they are old they will not depart from Your ways. Amen.

Scripture References:
Matthew 9:37–38   Romans 6:11
2 Corinthians 6:2   Proverbs 22:6

Prayers for—Godly Leadership

Prayer for Christians Employed in Schools

*...Single men in the night will be more likely to
ascertain facts than the best glasses in the day.*
George Washington – To Anthony Wayne, July 10, 1776

Lord Jesus, I pray for those who already know You as their
Lord and Savior who work in this school. I come against a
spirit of fear and I ask for boldness for them to show the light
of the Gospel of Jesus to all those around them.

Give them divine appointments to share Your life with the
students, parents, and administrators.

Grant them wisdom so that they will know when to speak
and when to remain silent.

Let their light so shine that everyone around them will see
their good works and glorify You. Amen.

Scripture References:
2 Timothy 1:7   2 Corinthians 4:4
John 10:1–5   James 1:5
Matthew 5:16

Prayer for Godly Student Leaders

The closer you get to Jesus,
The less you need to promote yourself.
Rick Warren – <u>The Purpose Driven Life</u>

Dear Lord, I call forth student leaders who have the spirit of Joshua and Caleb—those who are not afraid to give a good report that the students in this school can and will turn against evil and seek after You with all their hearts.

Fill the student leaders with the spirit of wisdom and revelation in the knowledge of You.

I ask for leaders who are strong in You and in the power of Your might. Let them not compromise with the world but lift up a godly standard for others to follow.

I pray they put on the whole armor of God that they may be able to stand against all the evil tactics of the devil.

I pray for men and women of God to mentor and nurture student leaders in love and with accountability.

May they grow in favor with God and man. Amen.

Scripture References:
Deuteronomy 34:9   Ephesians 1:17
Ephesians 6:10–22   Titus 2:3–4Luke 2:52

Prayers for—Families

Prayer for Restoration of Families

The best thing a father can do for his children is to love his wife. Dr. James Dobson

Dear Lord Jesus, I pray for the families represented in this school. Turn the hearts of the parents to the children and the hearts of the children to their parents so there will not be any opposition or division in these families or a curse on our land.

Let discipline in the home be administered with love and respect so the children will not be provoked to rebellion and willfulness. Let the family members love each other and walk in forgiveness, bearing each other's burdens.

May the husbands love their wives as Christ loved His church and gave Himself for it. Let wives be submissive to their husbands and let the husbands take the leadership in the family in spiritual matters.

Let those parents who are believers live in such a way as to provoke their spouses and children to know You in a real and personal way.

I pray for the salvation of all the family members of the students in this school. Amen.

Scripture References:

Luke 1:17

Exodus 20:12

Genesis 12:3

Psalm 68:4–6

Malachi 4:5–6

1 Corinthians 7:14

Ephesians 5:22–24

Proverbs 15:27

Matthew 19:3–9

1 Corinthians 13:1–10

Ephesians 6:1–4

Acts 16:33–34

Prayer for Parents

*To give children a good education in manners, arts
and science, is important;
To give them a religious education is indispensable;
and an immense responsibility rests on parents and
guardians who neglect these duties.* Noah Webster

Father, I pray that the parents will discipline their children
and bring them up in the nurture and admonition of the Lord.
I ask that You strengthen the family unit and let the well-
being of the children take precedence over jobs and leisure
activities. Give the parents the determination to spend quality
time with their children. Let them attend to the affairs of their
household and see that the children do their homework and
that they come to school on time and ready to learn.

Let parents be supportive of the school and its policies. Let
parents require their children to be disciplined and respectful
of those in authority.

Let there be a moral fiber in the homes that parents would
honor their marriage vows. I pray for honesty and integrity in
each home as the parents honor You.

Raise up mothers and fathers who will intercede for their
children. Amen.

Scripture References:
1 Samuel 12:23–24
Acts 10
1 Timothy 5:8
1 Peter 2:13–15

Proverbs 13:24
Ephesians 6:4
James 1:19–21

Prayer for Single Parent Families

He [Jesus] was a member of the ten Boom family – it was just as easy to talk to Him as it was to carry on a conversation with my mother and father, my aunts, or my brother and sisters. He was there.
Corrie ten Boom – Thoughts on growing up

Dear Jesus, I ask that You would be the "missing parent" to the children who are in single parent families. Let the children know that You are looking after them, just as loving earthly parents would. May they know Your love and Your care throughout their lives. Protect the children who are in abusive situations. Expose every evil work of the devil in homes where physical or sexual abuse is happening.

Like the widow who came to Elisha because her sons were being taken into slavery due to the debt on their father, deliver all the children who are suffering from the bondages brought on them because of the sins and carelessness of their fathers and mothers. Provide for their financial needs and see that churches and people of God look after those without parents.

I come against a root of bitterness in any child who may harbor unforgiveness because a parent has left them or died. I pray that they will not blame You, Jesus, but rather that they will embrace Your love and divine direction for their lives.

Give them a heart to have a godly family of their own someday. Let them honor their father and mother that it may go well with them and that they may enjoy long life on the earth. Amen.

Scripture References:
Exodus 22:22–24

1 Samuel 1:26–28

1 Samuel 3:1–4:1

1 Kings 17:1–16

2 Kings 4:1–5

Psalm 68:5–6

Luke 7:11–15

Ephesians 6:2–3

2 Timothy 1:4–7

Prayers for—Morality

Prayer for Sexual Abstinence until Marriage

Among adolescents religiosity in the form of personal devotion and personal conservatism are highly correlated with low levels of onset substance use and abuse.
America's Youth: measuring the risk compiled by
The Institute for Youth Development, 2002

Dear heavenly Father, I come to You on behalf of the children in this school. I ask that sexual purity be established on this campus. Raise up a standard against the onslaught of the enemy that is coming against our children in the lie that is being presented that sexual expression is a way of life and that it is okay to have sex outside of marriage. I bind Satan; he has no right in this place, and he cannot promote his lies on this campus. Let fornication, all uncleanness, and covetousness not be named in this place.

Bring forth godly teachers who will teach abstinence. Let our children learn patience in waiting until marriage to engage in sexual activity. Let them learn the fear of the Lord and that ungodly actions have negative consequences.

I pray for godly curriculum that will teach the children to live clean lives before You and desire Your perfect will for their lives and for their future families.

Let there be an intense hunger and thirst for righteousness on this campus because Your Word says that then they will be filled with joy and peace and all the other good things that come with Your righteousness. Amen.

Scripture References:
Isaiah 59:19
Matthew 18:18–20
Romans 6:23–7:1
Ephesians 4:27
Matthew 5:6

Prayer for Honesty When Taking Tests and Doing Homework

The first ideal that the child must acquire in order to be actively disciplined
is that of the difference between good and evil; and the task of the educator lies in seeing that the child does not confound good with immobility and evil with activity. Maria Montessori

Dear heavenly Father, I pray for a spirit of honesty and integrity to be prevalent in this school. You said that we should not steal, and I ask that there be no stealing of intellectual material in this school. May every student be responsible for his own homework and tests. Let it be a disgrace to steal or for one student to share her work with someone else.

Your Word says that if we are honest and faithful in the little things, You will make us ruler over much. Bring forth leaders, as they are honest in homework and test taking.

Reveal those things that are hidden and give teachers, counselors, and administrators wisdom as they deal with students who are cheating.

With the onslaught of the enemy to try to persuade our children that cheating is okay, raise up a godly standard that will give those who are tempted the ability to stand up and say no. Amen.

Scripture References:
Exodus 21:15
Proverbs 12:17
Luke 16:10
James 1:5

Prayer for Freedom from Homosexual Agenda

When God looks at a man or a woman,
He sees the promise of seed and the hope of generations,
a seed with the potential to continue its preordained purpose
to crush Satin's head.
Dr. Pat Morgan – How to Raise Children of Destiny

Father, I pray that You would create within each student a desire to grow up and have a godly family, and that through that godly union, all the families in the earth would be blessed. Let each child and adult in this school desire a life of being blessed by having a spouse of the opposite sex.

I ask for forgiveness for anyone who is caught in the sin of homosexuality. Translate them from the kingdom of darkness into the kingdom of Your dear Son. May a holy fear of You come over everyone in this building so that they will reverence You and live free from the sin of homosexuality.

I ask that the fathers and mothers of these children be convicted if they are involved in any form of pornography or sexual perversion. Expose these sins if those involved refuse to repent. Let those magazines, TV shows, videos, Internet sites, and books that promote homosexuality no longer be profitable because of lack of demand.

I pray that our school systems would acknowledge You as the Creator of the heavens and the earth, and as we acknowledge You, then the children of our land would not turn to the sin of homosexuality. Amen.

Scripture References:
Genesis 12:1–3
Proverbs 14:27
Proverbs 24:1–2
Ephesians 5:8–14
Romans 1:18–2:1
Colossians 1:13–14
2 Thessalonians 3:1–5
1 Peter 3:12

Prayer for Those Who Have Had an Abortion and Those Who Are Considering Having an Abortion

For God to use your painful experiences, you must be willing to share them.
Rick Warren – <u>The Purpose Driven Life – What on Earth Am I Here For?</u>

Dear Lord Jesus, You hold each one of us in the palm of Your hand and You care so much about everyone that You even know the number of hairs on our heads.

I ask Your forgiveness for every woman in this school who has had an abortion. Forgive their sin of murder, even if it was caused by fear. I also ask for forgiveness for the sin of selfishness where it has caused someone to abort a child.

Let the righteous intervene on behalf of any unborn child where the mother is contemplating having an abortion.

You said that if Your people would seek Your face and turn from our wicked ways, You would forgive our sins and heal our land. Now I pray that this country would turn from its wicked ways and ban abortion. Hear my cry for those who cannot speak for themselves. In Jesus name I pray. Amen.

Scripture References:
Exodus 20:13   Leviticus 18:21
Ezekiel 33:7–9   2 Chronicles 7:13–14
Proverbs 31:8–9

Prayer for Those Caught in Addictions

Twenty-five percent of the children of divorce reported using illicit drugs and alcohol before age 14, compared with 9% of the comparison group.
America's Youth: measuring the risk by The Institute for Youth Development

Dear Father, I pray for those children who are caught in a web of deception with habits and behaviors that are addictive. Jesus, You said that You came to set the captives free and now I ask for that freedom to reign in the life of every child in this school.

I cry out for help for each child who is bound by drugs, alcohol, eating disorders, or sexual sins. Let them come in contact with counselors, godly youth leaders, pastors, and caring Christians who will have compassion and will speak to them in a way that the bondages will have to go.

Heal past hurts and allow Your healing power to come into their lives.

I ask this in Your Name, Jesus. Amen.

Scripture References:
Psalm 5:2   John 14:13
Romans 6:18   Galatians 5:1

Prayer for—The Curriculum of Schools

Prayer for School Curriculum

*The philosophy of the schoolroom in one generation
will be the philosophy of government in the next.*
Abraham Lincoln

Father, I come before You in the mighty name of Jesus on
behalf of the curriculum that is being taught in our schools. I
ask that all teaching be in accordance with sound doctrine
and that the students will learn to say no to ungodliness and
worldly passions and live self-controlled, upright, and godly
lives. Let there not be greed on the part of those who produce
teaching materials but let their motives be to produce godly
character in the students. Let those who know You be
discerning in every situation and not receive or pass on
material that teaches children to disobey their parents or
promote senseless, faithless, heartless, and ruthless behavior.
May Your children choose Your instruction instead of silver,
knowledge rather than choice gold. Let there be a hatred of
what is evil in Your sight and a love for the things You love.

May all curriculums bless You and Your people so that You
will make this nation great and will bless us.

I pray that the false religion of humanism would be exposed
for the lie that it is. I ask for godly curriculum writers to
come forth—those who will be the salt of the earth and the
light of the world. May they be as a city on a hill that cannot
be hidden.

May our children be as Daniel who praised You for Your
wisdom and power. May You reveal deep and hidden things

to our children and give them knowledge and understanding in all kinds of literature and learning. I pray this in Your Name. Amen.

Scripture References:

Genesis 12: 2–3

Numbers 22:9

1 Samuel 2:30

Job 12:13

Proverbs 8: 12–21

Daniel 1:17

Daniel 2:19-23

Matthew 8:36

Matthew 5:13–16

Luke 12:15

Romans 1:28–32

Romans 12:9

Colossians 3:5–10

Titus 2:1–2

2 Peter 2:1–3

1 John 2:27

Prayers—of Repentance

Prayer of Repentance for Allowing Evolution to Be Taught in Our Schools

Evolution is at the basis of modern public education where the child is taught that he is an animal linked by evolution to the monkeys.
Samuel Blumenfeld <u>NEA – Trojan Horse in American Education</u>

Dear Father in heaven, the Creator of heaven and earth, I come to You on behalf of all the parents, educators, and children and repent for allowing the story of Your creation to be taken out of the curriculum of our schools. Forgive us and our forefathers. We have been fools because we have said there is no God. Forgive the judges of this land as they represented us when they struck down the teaching of Your creation. We have allowed a spirit of perversion to come upon our land; forgive us and turn our country back to You.

Now Lord, I acknowledge You, the One true and living God who created man in Your own image that we should serve and worship You. Let a Spirit of truth about You and Your marvelous plan of creation rise up in this school. Let the orderliness of the universe and the marvels of creation speak out in the classrooms. Let those who reverence You solemnly declare You as the Creator of mankind and of the universe. Amen.

Scripture References:
2 Kings 16:2–4
Romans 1:17–21
Acts 4:12
Psalm 51:3–4
Genesis 3:12

Prayer of Repentance for Allowing Prayer to Be Taken Out of Our Schools

Without God there is not virtue because there is no
prompting of the conscience;
Without God there is a coarsening of the society;
Without God democracy will not and cannot long endure.
If we ever forget that we are One Nation Under God,
then we will be a Nation gone under.
President Ronald Reagan

Father, I come before You in repentance and ask Your forgiveness for allowing prayer to be taken out of our schools. Even though I was not personally there when this happened, I am repenting for those who followed Jesus, but turned the other way. Forgive us of our apathy and lack of political involvement. Forgive us for our lack of personal prayer and devotion to Jesus and to His ways.

You said that men ought to always pray and to not give up. Forgive us for giving up a life of prayer and restore our schools.

Lord, as we have reaped the results of forsaking Your ways, hear my prayer and turn the hearts of the students in this school toward You. Amen.

Scripture References:
Psalm 79:9–10   Luke 18:18

Prayer of Repentance for Allowing Humanism to Be the Religion of Our Schools

There is a great danger of a final, and we believe fatal, identification of the word religion with the doctrines and methods which have lost their significance and which are powerless to solve the problem of human living in the Twentieth Century.
Humanist Manifesto

Dear heavenly Father, You sent us the Spirit of Truth that would protect us from deception. I ask that the Spirit of Truth reveal the spirit of lawlessness and the great deception of Humanism to parents, teachers, students, and administrators. I pray that these children would measure themselves against Your law and not against their peers. Keep our children from the delusion that there is no accountability for their sins. Teach Your children that You are their Father and that You watch over each one of Your children.

I ask that You reveal the lies of those who have deceived our educational system through the years. You said that the eyes of the Lord would be on the righteous and You would be attentive to our prayers, but the memory of the unjust would be cut off from the earth.

Now to Him who sits on the throne and to the Lamb of God be praise and honor and glory and power, forever and ever! Amen.

Scripture References:
Numbers 23:19
1 Kings 21:20–26
Psalm 34:15–16
Psalm 92:11–15
Romans 1:21–2:1
2 Corinthians 10:12
2 Thessalonians 2:9–17
1 John 2:22–23
1 John 4:4–6
Revelation 5:11–6:1

Prayer of Repentance for Allowing the Bible to Be Taken Out of Schools

Let the children...be carefully instructed in the principles and obligations of the Christian religion. This is the most essential part of education. The great enemy of the salvation of man, in my opinion, never invented a more effectual means of extirpating (removing) Christianity from the world than by persuading mankind that it was improper to read the Bible at schools. Benjamin Rush

Father, I repent on behalf of my nation, America, for allowing the Bible to be removed from our classrooms. I ask You to forgive us that no one was there to stand in the gap and pray and believe You for the Bible to remain in our schools, so that our children could quote Your Word, say Your prayers, and reference Your Word as truth in their research papers.

May Your Word, once again, be a lamp unto the feet of our children and a light unto their path. Let Your Word be the moral compass that will guide the children into right standing with You and with their peers.

Lord, I have watched as our national test scores have gone down and our children have become an object of scorn, a byword among the nations. May we call a sacred assembly and a fast to cause our school system to once again acknowledge You.

As the students in this school meditate in Your Word, let them become creative, perceptive, intelligent, and spiritually motivated. I ask this in the Name of Jesus. Amen.

Scripture References:
2 Chronicles 6:25
2 Chronicles 7:14
Joshua 1:8
Psalm 119:105
Ezekiel 22:30
Acts 2:38
Hebrews 4:12

Prayer for—Racial Harmony

Prayer for Racial Harmony in Our Schools

Jesus loves the little children,
All the children are His care;
Red and yellow, black and white,
They are precious in His sight;
Jesus loves the little children everywhere.
Theo Harris – "Jesus Loves the Children"

Father, I pray for harmony between all the races represented in this school. Let all bickering, fighting, and contention be ended. Let each race walk together in harmony and in love with other races. Let the different streams of the nations come together with camaraderie and unity. Where there is hate replace it with Your love and understanding.

I ask that a spirit of pride be bound and that in its place would be a spirit of humility.

I pray that each student would follow Your admonition to do to others as they would have others do to them. Amen.

Scripture References:
Psalm 133:1   Luke 6:31
John 17:23   1 Peter 5:5

Prayer for—Revival

Prayer for Revival in Our Schools

Brother, if you are to win that province you must go forward on your knees.
Hudson Taylor – Missionary to China

Father, may the children in this school not only hear the name of Jesus but may they know You personally. May they know the Jesus who came to give them eternal life and an abundant life in this earth. Sweep away religious baggage and let them learn to love the teachings of Your Son, Jesus. Let them serve Him alone.

Just as when Jonah went to Nineveh and proclaimed the Word of the Lord, send prophets to this school and to this nation to proclaim Your Word to us today. Prepare the hearts of the students to hear what You have to say to them. Let the seed of Your Word fall on good soil.

I pray for a complete moral and spiritual revival in this school and across this land. May the students here be so on fire for You that they will be a city set on a hill that cannot be hidden. Amen.

Scripture References:
Jonah 1:1- 3   Habakkuk 3:2
Luke 8: 5–8   John 10:10
Matthew 5:14

Prayer for—Our Students to Be Patriotic

Prayer for Patriotism in Our Students

That patriotism, which catching its inspiration from the immortal God, animates and prompts to deeds of self-sacrifice, of valor, of devotion, and of death itself – that is public virtue, that is the sublimest of all public virtues.
Henry Clay

Father, in the name of Jesus, I lift up the students in this school, and I ask that You would give them a love for their country, America. Let them be willing to serve their country at home and abroad. Let them know that freedom did not come without a price.

I pray for textbooks, curriculum, and teachers who would teach the values of America and not tear it down.

Let the children rise up like David's mighty men who stood their ground and defeated the enemy. Amen.

Scripture References:
2 Samuel 23:8–12   Deuteronomy 4:9
2 Chronicles 26:10

Prayers of—Thanksgiving

Prayer of Thanksgiving for Our Country

Liberty cannot be preserved without general knowledge among the people.
John Adams

Dear heavenly Father, I am so grateful to You for this wonderful land of America. Thank You for the rich godly heritage we have in this country.

Thank You for the foundations that were laid by our forefathers, who had insight into Your Word and established a government that gives us freedom to worship as we wish and freedom to be what we want to be.

Thank You for the heroes who have given their lives so that we might live in freedom.

Thank You for bringing those to this country who believed in the integrity of Your Word and who wanted future generations to be able to know You. Without their insight we would have been subjected to tyranny.
I will praise Your Name for the great freedoms and You have given in this great land of America. Amen.

Scripture References:
Psalm 8:1   Psalm 25:3
Jeremiah 29:11

Prayer of Thanksgiving for Our Schools

Where there is no vision, the people perish.
Proverbs 29:18

Thank You, Father, for providing a school system in this country that allows each child an opportunity to learn. Thank You for textbooks and teaching materials that are interesting and that make learning fun.

Thank You for the years when the educational system taught Your Word as truth and established the teaching and precepts of Your Son, Jesus, as truth to the children.

Thank You for teachers who often work long, hard hours to help our children. Thank You for our colleges and universities that train the teachers and administrators to be effective educators.

Thank You for giving our founding fathers foresight in establishing an educational system that would make not only this country great, but that would be a blessing to the whole world. I am grateful that those early generations saw that the young minds of our country were its greatest natural resource. Amen.

Scripture References:
Psalm 30:12
Psalm 107:1

Psalm 95:2
1 Peter 1:18

About the Author

Nancy Huff is a former teacher who taught in public and private schools for 13 years. She has a bachelor's degree in mathematics and a master's degree in English as a second language.

Nancy is founder and president of Teach the Children International (TCI), a non-profit organization that reaches out to children at risk in the United States and abroad.

TCI sponsored a program for schools in America called "Take a Walk That Will Change Eternity." The goal is to have every school in America covered by on-site prayer every day that school is in session. TCI has sponsored two citywide calls to prayer for the schools in the Tulsa, Oklahoma area. The purpose of this call is to encourage individuals, churches, and organizations to intercede for specific schools.

Overseas, Nancy has helped to start a school for Sudanese refugees. Her organization, TCI, provides humanitarian relief, school supplies, and outreach programs for refugee children..

Nancy writes magazine articles and books about education and children's issues to raise awareness and promote public involvement in the needs of children. She is a speaker on prayer and children's ministry at conferences around the country. Amen.

Contact Us

To receive updated material on how to pray for America's Educational System and more scriptural prayers and prophetic declarations go to TeachTheChildrenInternationa.com and sign up for our newsletter.

Other books by Nancy Huff:

<u>**Taking the Mountain of Education: A Strategic Prayer Guide for American Education**</u>

<u>**How to Create Passive Income with Rental Property**</u>

<u>**A Call to Prayer for Children Teens and Young Adults in the 10/40 Window**</u>

Available on Amazon.com

Nancy Huff
Teach the Children International
P.O. Box 700832
Tulsa, OK 74170-0832

(918) 369-5081(tel)
(918) 512-4618 (fax)

E-mail: contactTCI@aol.com

Web Site:
TeachTheChildrenInternational.com

Made in the USA
Las Vegas, NV
14 October 2021